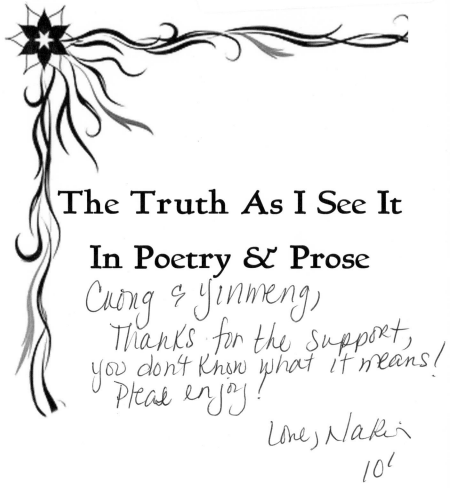

# The Truth As I See It

## In Poetry & Prose

Cuong & Yinmeng,
Thanks for the support,
you don't know what it means!
Please enjoy!

Love, Nakia

10'

**Nakia R. Laushaul**

For more information, contact Serendipity Bound Books, 12620 FM 1960 West Suite A Box 121 Houston, TX 77065


Scriptures taken from the HOLY BIBLE, NEW INTERNATIONAL VERSION®. Copyright © 1973, 1978, 1984 Biblica. Used by permission of Zondervan. All rights reserved.

*Library of Congress Control Number:* **2009911618**

ISBN **978-0-9843682-6-6**


*Todd Needom* cover art and design
*Aaron Hinskston III* back cover design

Photo by Todd Needom appears on page 28.
Photo by *Quyen Le* appears on page 147.
Photo by *Jovante Tunon* appears on page 62.
Photo by *Derrick Mitchell appears on* page 39.
Photos by *Nakia Laushaul* appear on pages 24 and 121.

# Acknowledgements

First, I'd like to thank my son, J. Tunon. Before you, love was only a figment of my imagination. You have made me a better person than I could have ever been without you in my life. It's all about you baby!

My family (ALL of Y'all), where I come from is who I am. Grandma Ethel, you cover all the ground you stand on. Me too! Hawkins, words are no use, just love. You are the epitome of the word – Family.

My Rafiki, my amigos (Dev, Susan, Isa, & Lam). Had it not been for you, where oh where would I be? You have encouraged me (Brooke, Catherine, Arnette, Felicia, Tamika, & Joanna), prayed with me (Ms. D), assisted me (Todd, Tonja, & Angela) and pushed me to do what my heart desires. To others looking for your names; You know who you are which is far more meaningful than if I listed all of you for the world to see. If I missed you, go ahead and write your name right here _____. You should already know that it's written in my heart.

My fellow writers, whether I met you on a busy street corner in Harlem, amongst the dazzling lights of Las Vegas (BWRC 09), chatting it up online, or if I read your book and couldn't get your characters out of my head, thank you. When I didn't know my next move, I could always call on you (Marguerite Benjamin Parker, Monique D. Mensah, & Sophia Simmons). You made this process look so easy; I dared to think I could. And I did.

Thank you Pastor Phillip Powell of San Bernardino Christian Center, where I learned to seek God on my own. Pastor Remus Wright of The Fountain of Praise, where I learned to worship like I'm grown.

Lord, thank you for breaking me open, filling me up with wisdom, and seamlessly stitching me back together again. I get it Lord, the lights are on and my heart is full. Thank you for taking my hand and entrusting me with your words. You are the truth. Everything is for You.

# Table of Contents

INTRODUCTION

## PART ONE
### The Truth As I See It about You and Me

## PART TWO
### The Truth As I See It about Love

## PART THREE
### The Truth As I See It about God

## PART FOUR
### The Truth As I See It About Life

The Trials of Raising a Man

# Introduction

I love the written word. Ever since I was nine years old I knew that I wanted to write. I still remember the first real book I ever read, and the impact that novel still has over my life. Somehow, life, love, and discontentment squeezed itself in between the coils of God's purpose for my existence. I buried my dreams. Whatever the case, it doesn't matter anymore. What is important is that I am here now and oh how happy I am to be exactly where I am, introducing myself to you. I commit to the integrity of my thoughts soulfully arranged on paper. I know this is the first you may have heard of me, but it won't be the last.

This is my dream, not to write poetry, but to tell stories. Stories that bruise, scab over, and finally heal as though there was never a bruise. There were so many nights I lay awake crying and thinking about what it really meant to be a woman, a mother, a sister, a daughter, a member of society, and most importantly a child of God. I thought it was insomnia (smile), but it was purpose calling out to me. Finally, I put pen to paper and I let my fingers tap incessantly across my keyboard until the joy and pain within poured out of my spirit.

I offer to you my stories in the form of poetry & prose.

This is The Truth As I See It.

*If you think this book is all about me, pay close attention as some of it is all about you.*

*Love, Nakia*

# The Truth As I See It

## *About You and Me*

# Part One

# Invisible Ink

I am going to pour all my pain out into this pen.
I am going to pour all my hope out into this pen.
Drain it to the very end.
Write, until it seeps into invisibility.
And I am free
        And she is free
                And he is free.

# Presenting Me

I present to me—Me
Never looked at myself in this fashion
Sort of feeling this brand new self attraction
Excited about my extra personal affair
I'm so becoming to myself
From my cute toes up to my last thread of hair
Can't explain what is happening to me
My attitude in sync with my true being
It's all aligning
I feel God smiling
I would now like to introduce you
To the all new self improved—Me

# I Am A Tree

Why does everyone want to change me?

    Change the way I think

    Change the way I react

    Change the way I talk

    Change the way I feel

Don't they know I am a TREE Dammit?

I cannot be moved. Only pruned.

My wild untamed branches shaved back.

Tangles trimmed and properly put into place.

Only grow wild again another day.

I am happy being me.  A TREE!

| | | | |
|---|---|---|---|
| Unmovable | Unstoppable | Opinionated | Motivated |
| Beautiful | Sexy | Soft | Tall |
| Moral | Wild | Outspoken | Sassy |
| Honest | Proud | Coarse | Resilient |
| Rugged | Strong | | |

I am Intense.

I am Fierce.

I am the Shelter and the Shade.

My bark is so raw.

My sap bleeds confidence.

Look at me in all my brown radiance.

I am in love with me. A TREE.

All full grown.

A TREE stands alone.

Sometimes when I look around – look around – look around.

I see a few other TREEs like me standing Tall and Proud.

Yet, I've watched as even more TREEs like me have succumbed to the simple ways of this world and been cut down!

That's when I go into full protection mode.

I'm talking terminal damage control will be very necessary if you shake me.

The only things soft about me are my supple roots,

That's why I buried those miles and miles underground.

Go ahead. I'll stand here.

Chop one down.

I'll just sprout another. And you can't stand it.

See you don't understand,

my roots are the only thing keeping this TREE standing.

Hey. Hey. You in the jungle watch out for this TREE

Because if mishandled, I will let one of my mighty branches fall,

Encase you in a root and crush you.

    Your mind    your spirit    and your will.

I am not afraid. I am a TREE.

TREEs don't run.

They stand still.

TREEs are born free.

Live free. Die free.

Shit, I know secretly you want to be a TREE just like me.

Come on. Think about it.

Think real hard and tell me the last time you heard a TREE apologize for being a TREE.

Tell me what else you know that's as bad ass as me.

That has the possibility to stand outside.

In the stone cold *alone*.

Naked of my leaves.

And still have the audacity not to hide behind anything.

I am a TREE.

A fucking TREE.

You can't change me!

# The Immortal Me

When I die, I'm already born again
Worry about me, honey please
Throw my ashes into an empty field
Grow me again, reincarnated into a field of weeds
From dust to an exhilarating rush and back to ashes
Choke on me
I am nothing
Until you make me exist again
Let my tears roll off this page
     My sorrow
Rest in your lap
     My laughter
Finger snaps. More.
Hand claps. More.
Go ahead. Holler.
Cry, get pissed but please agree
Listen. This is all of me
Read the iridescent lines that attempt to hide
The road to divinity
Believe me
As DNA evaporates
Disintegrates into the atmosphere
Conjoining into emaciated air
And fades away
I am exhumed

Inhaled by you
My immortality belongs with you
I bequeath my thoughts, my words, my sound, my voice
Receive my spirit
Allow me to live forever in your seed
Intertwine our family history
Write my name on your family hierarchy.
I belong to you
I am immortal
My work is done
The doors of Heaven are open, for me.

# I Am Not Afraid

I am not afraid
I conquered fear a long time ago
I stood in my closet surrounded by weeping skeletons
Ferocious ghosts from ancestors past
Weary from their weight
I carried their burdens
So, I packed
I packed them
Laid them to rest
Neatly in respective graves
Oh, how I prayed
Prayed over restless souls

I am not afraid
Of me anymore

# Dance

Can you hear the music?
It's not all in your head.
The angels are humming.
The universe is strumming.
Time has been suspended.
Everything.
Everyone is waiting for you.
It's your solo.
What should you do?
Silly questions.
Silly you.
Hold your own hand,
That's what you have two for.
Take your rightful position.
The center of the floor.
Dance with a purpose.
Dance. Dance.
Until you can't dance anymore.

# *Obligated*

I close my eyes with thoughts of you.

My life revolves around

     Who will you be one day?

Only half of my dreams are for me.

     Maybe Less.  What are you dreaming?

Dare I dream of dreams long past.

I vaguely remember those selfish days filled with selfish ways.

I live through you.  I live for you.

 I tiptoe to your bedside while you are sleeping

     picking up your things, ironing your clothes, scrutinizing

     your homework, scheduling your life.

"Are you using your time wisely?" I wonder.

     Take all the time you need to dream the impossible.

     It's possible.

I progressively heave my existence forward.

     Is Mommy getting better?

Sorry I stole a few moments from time
      You caught me.  You needed me.  I am learning.
Time is never recaptured.
This is a struggle.
Your being is a gift I have given you.
Half of me. For all of you
You are welcome.

# *Liberated*

Pro Choice!
Pro Choice!
Women have the right to choose!
If we won something,
Then who did we lose?
14th Amendment protects no embryos.


Naive little girls, mimicking videos
No date rape
She said okay
One new bastard on the way
   She doesn't want it
Runway, here I come
My dreams are in L.A.
All the daddies said no way
I'm not liable, viable, or reliable
Not yet anyway.
Got my scholarship.
Gonna shoot off like a rocket,
   Someday . . .
Take Daddy's money and Run!
Mom said, Go, Quick!
Son, talk her into it.
Little lives just begun,
Inside her stomach—that doesn't count.

A protected smoking gun
Rounds of unlimited ammunition
Passed on from a secret sorority
With no hesitation
And they call it li-ber-ty. For me.
Pro Choice!
Pro Choice!
Babies have the right to die
Sorry baby.
Maybe *you* can choose another Mommy
Come back some other time and apply

# To My Child
## (for JT)

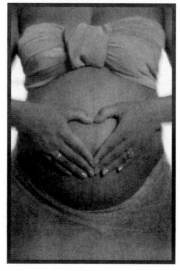

I was supposed to teach you how to love.

I know.

I was supposed to build your character.

I know.

I was supposed to instill pride in you.

I know.

I was supposed to nurture your confidence.

I know.

I was supposed to shield you from the evil in the world.

I know.

But you, my child born of my womb have shown me all these things.

You are amazing.

# Cute, Little Baby

You are my chocolate chip
Sweet honey dip
Marinated and flavored
Blended perfectly!

Kissed by the sun

Oh, how God has blessed
The universe with you
Little beautiful one

# Happy Mother's Day

I hate going to church on Mother's Day!
I love my mom, don't get me wrong.
I just hate going to church on Mother's Day!
To sit and listen to all the things I'd been missing.
For hours on end makes me cringe.
Everybody doesn't have the ultimate matriarch experience.
Church on Mother's Day reminds me of this.
I'm clapping, so unhappy.
Lying and pretending.
Depression sinks in.
I feel ten again.

My son is here with me.
I'm doing the right thing
Self, don't lose focus.
Come back to reality.
Why is everybody staring at me?
Damn, I forgot to keep clapping
  I don't look happy.
I hate church on Mother's Day . . . Father's Day too!

# Thanks Father

Home grown from his tears.

Watered down with his fears.

Heavy rage belonging to my father

I swallow it,

It consumes me.

Hate seizes my soul.

Bleeding an ocean of moans,

Experiences blinded by salt.

Drowning in bitter memories.

My wonderful legacy.

# Not My Problem

How dare I be happy
Rain spits on my parade

Thunder bolts
Electricity jolts

Threaten my incomplete being
Dare I laugh
Hiding behind sheets of rain
My sister's anguish is also my pain

# Leaning Tree
### (Hawkins Family)

You are my family
My leaning tree
Extended and uninhibited
No pain intended
I need your unconstrained love
Psyche world weary
I wipe my eyes on the leaves of my leaning tree
I run to you
Whenever I need to
Open arms greet me
Emotions release
Until, I am calm
Again, I draw strength from you
Ready, again to make the world weary
You are my family
My leaning tree

# Sherbet

I'm the darkest face in the crowd.
Laughing loud.
Teeth shining.
Didn't know til later,
Or didn't care,
A Polaroid captured our unanimous joy.

Still smiling.
Looking at my closest friends,
We blend
Nicely! Into Sherbet.

# My Rafiki
### (to all my girls, too many to count)

i love to delight in your happiness
    you, my priceless treasure to behold
    My Friend,
    with an essence, so benevolent
    it humbles me to be the
    desire of your presence
    i am here,
    not merely to share the joy in your life
    i pray you through the tumultuous times
    it thrills me when you seek me
    to wipe tears from your eyes
    i am here,
    if you drop a single tear
    i cry a puddle
    we have each other
    only the lonely cry alone
    you, My Friend
    need only,
    pick up the phone

i love to hold your hand
    linking perfectly across distant lands
    from far to right here
    My Friend, My Companion

in Portuguese and in Spanish
you are My Amigo
and in Italian, My Amico
my life is dull
only amusing
not when i,
but when We go
together, wherever
you are the spice of my life,
adding ethnic flavor to my spirit,
arousing me with our cultural difference
the language of love
calls you My Ami,
in Swahili, you are My Rafiki
My Friend,
reach for me,
dance with me

i love to multiply you by life
    if i retrace steps
    from all my stages
    i continuously add faces
    you keep coming,
    i keep growing
    we keep dividing
    i'm giddy from multiplying
    until i forget
    who knew who and when
    or how, forget why

My Friend,
what's significant
is not who came first
at last, i finally met you
totally enamored
by the beautiful memories
i hold sacred in my heart
til breath determines
our very end
you, me
We are Friends

Spanish - Amigo        Italian- Amico

Polish - Przyjaciel        Turkish - Arkadas

French - Ami        Mandarin - Pengyou

Norwegian - Venn        Danish - Veninde

German- Freund        Irish - Cara

Dutch - Vriend        Scottish - Caraid

Swahili - Rafiki        Zulu - Umngane

Hindi - Mitr lighter

# Sister Strength

Keep beating my head against the same log
Bracing myself, waiting for the world to fall
Pacing the floor, back and forth all night
Like imperceptible pain, something is just not right
Like a check book that a crook took
I'm checking my achievement balance
I'm in the negative,
Time to take a stance
This is possibly my last chance
Failure is fast on my heels
Rapidly becoming a blur in the rear
No matter how tempting,
I refute death by fear
I keep gaining distance
I am not permitted to stop
No time to steal a breath
Self-esteem keeps me in check
Efforts to swarm me and harm me uncovered
Friends take no pay for high rank in an opposing army
My Sister Strength assumes position and defeats my enemy

I penetrate invisible doors all day
Always moving and proving
Keeping minutes of the games they play
Until all my energy is spent
Constantly seeking and peeking around corners
In anticipation of a peace of mind
A place to get rejuvenated
Reinvigorated
Is very hard to find with this dark skin
And genitalia of mine
Infiltrating the dividing line uninvited

Oblivious of the pompous looks I get
I persist to stay put, because I deserve it
My Sister Strength has demonstrated I am worth it

I hate repetition not to mention-reiteration
Cries echo through iron windows anyway
The universe is whispering
Two words are my lonely ammunition
Against the heavy cruelty
The massive responsibility
Passed on
Pressed down inside of me
Though trials suffocate my community
Only I, am not permitted to stop
Even a clock at times, runs out
Ceases to exist, ceases to tick
In a master plan of cruel tricks
My Sister Strength won't synchronize with the word Quit.

# 5 W's and How: A Reality Check

**W**hen did we become a class that uplifts shakin ass
Our music filled with unrepeatable lyrics
We praise pimps and laugh at our own ignorance!
Don't think because we got a black president
He's gonna start passing out po' folks a check
Forgive our bourgie debt
Screw the rest of the country
It's all about you and me
The first thing y'all gone say is
Oh he forgot where he come from
It's really us, we've forgotten
How far we have come
Living dormant has become a real problem
This issue requires community involvement to solve it.
Are you with me yet?  Somebody needs a reality check.


**W**here you at mama
You're not at home raising your own babies,
Passing your kid from hand to hand
Running behind somebody else's man
Spending your check on the latest fit

Flipping food stamps to get rich quick
But, you spend it as fast as you get it
At the end of the month you still don't have fifty cents
That smooth dude that promised to take care of you
The one that made your coochie drool
He won't even buy you a peppermint after you used your mouth
Like a vise grip wrapped deliciously around his dick!
Are you with me yet?  Somebody needs a reality check.


**W**hat are you doing daddy that's so damn important
So sad you haven't seen your new baby boy yet,
He looks just like you,
Kid number two is 15 locked up in juvi
Forced to bend over and give up his precious young booty
You claim you were busy
Hmm,
Let's see spinning wheels in your souped up de ville,
        buying da bar,
        chasing skirts,
        popping collars,
        making money rain like it's a hurricane
Your 13 year old daughter is 5 months pregnant,
Hiding her black eye
Contemplating suicide
You stuck on pride
Turned a blind eye
Still mad at they mama

You have accountability as their father
Watch out you got a real treat coming from a bitch called Karma
Are you with me yet? Somebody needs a reality check.


**W**hy does grandma have pappas maybe and mamas baby?
Hell! she didn't even raise you to be a nice young lady
She get it from her mama
Ain't always a good thing to be passed down
Him being just like his daddy has led to all this tragedy
Insanity is raining on the black family
This is like a rewound scene of a bad movie stuck on stupidity
It just keeps on repeating and repeating
Nobody is taking responsibility
Little precious beings, nowhere to turn
End up just like us
Reliving this vicious cycle
Are you with me yet? Somebody needs a reality check.


**W**ho are you people that get to lay up all day smoking weed,
Never picked up a book to read,
Watching rated dumb sitcoms on BET
Or bootleg dvd's
Ever consider how this might misrepresent me in a bad light
I'm trying to raise my son right
All because it was so interesting
To watch Flava Flav fuck for a wife on VH1
It ever occur to you it's just another day

Another fast dollar
He pays child support for his sons
Please don't you see?
Rappers and actors are paid to feed you stupidity subliminally
TV is designed to make your mind subside, brain cells die
Across the world little boys in Africa
Screaming out the N word,
    committing genocide,
    taught to self hate,
    depreciate human value
Mimicking a fake gansta fool
Thanks to that homemade video you thought was cool
to post on YouTube
You don't really think do you!
Because they bleeped out explicit lyrics
Imaginary beams via an MTV satellite stream
The world is asleep and too blind to see
We lost focus of our goals and dreams
Oh, my bad you never had time to set any,
So focused on watching other people
Live out their dreams on reality TV
Are you with me yet? Somebody needs a reality check.


How do we get the original black back?
They had real class
They would all get together and ride on that ass
North and South
East and West

They got exactly what they came for. Justice
Heads held high, Fists pumpin pride
What had happened was
We got off the damn bus,
Got a little taste of money and it changed all of us
Us. Collectively should begin again
Act like we got some sense again
Start within your own strong black family
We can all reap the rewards of real prosperity
Integrity. Only minds set free can see
Endless possibilities stretched back from history into infinity!
Each one of us that can reach one of us has the responsibility
Teach another one of us
It's time to save us!
It's time to fade front to black
Are you still with me?

# Philosophic

People don't want the real you
Happy people pretend to be someone new
I want to be like them
Accommodating.
Obliging.
Hiding actually, from the authentic me

We never say precisely what we are thinking
Expectations answer in lieu of what we are dreaming

This is confusing
Perplexing.
Bewildering that I am not who I think I am
Am I?

# Takers

The more you give,
the more they take
The more you share,
the more they hoard
The more you allow

You disappear

# Mirror, Mirror on the Wall

Look closely
Closer
Now Focus!

Object in mirror
Is who it appears to be
It's you

Sorry, it's not what you wanted
Your reflection
To say about you!
Me, either.

# Let Me Out

i can not be confined
by the human mind
indivisible
i am a spirit
floating
in a paradise
that i own
unlocked
to roam
amorous
wholly unleashed
existing
merely if
I am free

# Move Now

I am a gentle force
Swelling, with no outlet
Growing
Growing
Growing
Move out of the way
I'm about to burst
Growing
Growing
Growing
I was a gentle mist
I am a tidal wave

I told you to move out of the way

# *Who is They?*

Been looking for them,
Them, or this mysterious They for a long time
Time flew past and i lost the opportunity to fulfill my destiny
Destiny deterred, stinking in pseudo reality
Reality set in while i proclaimed busy
Busy hunting for They
They, meanwhile, must have snatched my destiny away
Or foolishly did i give it away, because who exactly is *They*?

# Welcome to Your Life

Welcome to the rest of your life
No longer Mama's baby,
Daddy's big boy.
After years of oblivious joy,
Time demands
Turn away your childhood toys
You have graduated
Moved into the unfamiliar
Careful, it's the abyss of maturity
Never alone
You are undaunted by the unknown
Steadfast in what you already know
You, beautiful one
Are always within earshot of God
Hey, young man.
Mr. Decision Maker
Go. Fly. Run. Leap
Rise baby Rise
Now is not the time to sleep
Smell it
It's coming fast at you
Oh, sweet success
Snatch it
Grab at it

Say you, young son
Stick out your tongue!
Taste the victories
Eat them whole
Get full of life in your soul
With pre-empted footsteps
Weighted by confidence
Make the earth rattle and quake
At your reach
Imprint your name
It's your entitlement.
Welcome to the new realm of your life.

## *Peaceful Destinations*

A gentle breeze
Spawned by a wave of God's great hand
Peacefully.  Ascending towards relaxation,
    A well deserved retreat
Every few miles its path—crossed
In the attempt to quietly breeze by
    Movement prevented.  Progression and flow halted
Slothfulness wanted to capture it
Anger placed heavy demands on it,
Pride made the breeze feel guilty for being so free
Hindrances became nuisances
The Lord watched in tolerance,
    As it was up to the will of the breeze to
    Put a stop to it
There was no way around it,
Determination shaped it
Even the breeze knew,
Although it hated to
Straight through the obstacles
    Was the only way to go
Regretfully, the breeze made a decision,
It too had a mission, it was time
To focus less on being a welcome tickle,
A passing peaceful sway on a sweltering summer day
It turned and it twirled,

Leaving squeals of excuses
Insufficient apologies
Gusts of dismay
Swirling in the aftermath f tyranny
Later, everyone blamed the gentle breeze

And the moral of my poem is this:
A gentle breeze should never be taken lightly. Be considerate of the paths you cross and respectful when interrupting destinations.

## Temporis

Time is temporary
Ever evolutionary
Sever cluttered moments right away
As, every second you enter
Into a personal revolution again

# At Last

I've spent my life
Chasing mama
Chasing daddy
Chasing men
Chasing baby
Chasing friends
Chasing men
Chasing money
Chasing me

Finally,
I am free
Chasing dreams
I am happy

# *I Am Beautiful*

I FEEL BEAUTIFUL

When I feel God
When I feel loved
When I see J
When I am safe
When my clothes are on
When my shoes are off
When my hair is fly
When my lips are shiny
When my man is tall
When my wallet is fat
When I am kissed
When I write
When I sing
When I read
When I dream


I AM BEAUTIFUL

# The Truth As I See It

## *About Love*

## Part Two

# Blue

A lady sings the blues
Me too
I'm in a single funk
Capsized under a mountain of imaginary thoughts
Treading through life perfunctory
Having verbal intercourse with inanimate objects
My inner inconsistency is the only companion I get

And she sings the blues
Why does she get to sing the blues?
Well, I do too!

# No Limit

I can love you up close I can love you from the street I can love you from the car I can love you from a distance I can love you from no matter where you are. It's still the same love.

# Love in Focus

Though hidden from my eternity
Bliss almost passed me
Heart so broken I couldn't see
This love
This moment
This joy
This beautiful ache
Your kisses one by one mend my heart
Your love so simple, captivates me
Your love so fierce, twists and entwines me
Your love so blazing, burns passion ignite me
A deep yearning with no end
Love comes into sight
A heart this brand new
Can only focus on you
My love, I have you in plain sight

# Love Note: Lip Service

I watched you.
Your lips, especially.
I wondered if your kisses were sticky like honey.
If they dripped sweet like dew drops from a sinuate leaf.
I imagine they do,
If you used them on me
A flood of ecstasy would drown me
Rid me of my sanity.

Nervous, I retreat.
And so, from here I watch you
Your lips, especially.

# Heart One

Don't leave me standing out here alone
This is a place I've never been
My entire life I've looked for you
Your existence is my testament to truth

I'm trying to slow my pace
I want to run fast deep inside you
My heart pounds from fear
Be still heart, before he hears

Anticipation is making me sick
My vision blurred from excitement
Exhilaration makes me dizzy
Rational mind hurry, rescue me

Electrical currents running throughout
Shocks my sense of sensibility
I feel inside out
My core exposed to the elements
My wall neglected to protect it

I can't see anymore
I can't hear anyone
My heart bursts into a flame

I'm fighting blindly
I'm falling quickly

Heart one
Me none
Heart won
I'm in Love.

God's will be done.

# God sent you

I got lost more than once along the way
I am here
My heart blindly led
You are stunning
Separated by miles, vast like continents
I am found

A Love to behold with my heart
You are mine
My body embraces the lost rib
I am filled
Uninhibited ecstasy is realized
I am content
My nervous expectation begins
It is His will
He sent you

# *Brink of Submission*

You make me feel so vulnerable
Is this what it feels like to be a woman?
I mean,
I've been running nowhere doing my thing trying to help out
Everybody else, yeah most times
I've forgotten about myself
Lost a lot of my feminine wiles in this shuffle
Running ahead and foot into struggle
Don't really know how to be submissive
Does that word mean you will try to be the master over me?
At least that's what I heard could happen
If I let a man become the captain
I'm scared of us
Don't really know how to delegate trust
Not to mention chivalry
Baby please!
Born of a mother of the 50s
Don't forget rule number one
Always make sure that me
Can take care of me and we
And all the little us
Cause we can't depend on you
But when you said you loved me, it touched me
I started wondering
Is this something you could teach me?

Can a man teach a woman?
Who has been thoroughly conditioned
To think and act and speak
And hurt to push and pull
Yell, not trust to aggress
Stand, not sit to uphold myself
To finally let go
I inhale. Inhale. Twice.
Exhale once.
I can't. This is all I know.


You make me want to take to take chances I've never considered
Where do we start?
Tell me how do we begin?
Is there a manual on how to be a woman?
Filled with all the lessons I haven't been getting
Lets' start with the section about what I know of men
The story of my *generation of daddies* that didn't stick around
Some things are kinda hard to pick up
When you feel like you've been left to rot in the lost and found
You're not him are you?
Something about this thing lets me know that what you're offering
Just might be true and different and worth it
And healthy and oh so satisfyingly real
Is it time?
Should I try?
To go ahead and forgive all men
So you won't get convicted for their sins?

Please don't look to me
If you are the man God called you to be
I figured this, was the sort of thing you could show me
Can you? Will you?
Let's see if you noticed that this modern
Know it all . . . So together woman
Just requested your opinion
And. I respect it
Are you the damn deal?
Or is it all in my head?
My heart sure thinks you're him
Every night I go to bed, afraid to sleep
Don't want to find out God let my mind play a cruel trick on me
And you are only an illusion playing beautifully in my dreams
It might be time to let go.
I Inhale. Inhale. Twice.
Exhale once.
I want to.
This is all I know.


You make me forget everything I've been through
Your gentle words caress and soothe and protect me
Until I see God in you
I feel brand new
Like this is my first time
Like you are my first love
This is it isn't it?
How a woman should be treated

Like a delicate flower placed in the most exquisite vase
And set on display
You look at me like love has two eyes
All full of pride
Like I'm enough
Like one is better than twenty
Like *here* is exactly where you want to be
And you tell me. Repeatedly
Until love convinces me to believe you. What?
My heart is beating so thunderously loud
I don't think I heard you
Did you just say you believe in me too?
Maybe letting go of all the unnecessary information
Passed down from generation to generation
Was the only thing making this so complicated?
I Inhale. Inhale. Twice.
Exhale once.
I'm trying to let go of all I know.


You asked for my pain to melt into joy
My anger to trade for happiness
To provide when I fall short
When I am weak
You promised to be my strength
Whenever I am faced with disaster
You love me like Christ
So, *effortlessly*
This is right

I willingly give you the reigns to the wheel
I move over
I'm riding shotgun
It looks like you are self assured
And masculine enough
To be confident
About where we are going
You make me certain
You following God and likewise I follow you
Oh, this is the exact road love should travel
On cruise—no brakes—no acceleration
You driving,
Me giggling like a fool
Could this be what free, *feels like*?
I enjoy it so much
I don't have the desire to be every woman anymore
Nor the world's crutch
I just want to submit
And give and provide and nurture
And reinvent myself exclusively for you
I'm inhaling and exhaling.
Look at me.
I'm finally breathing.
Loving you is so easy.

# Divine Complements

From Heaven you were sent
You are my divine complement
Awaiting blissful ascension
Separated by invisible dimensions
The Holy Spirit confirmed
Power of connection embedded in His word
Mirrored from a borrowed rib
Familiarity lays in wait, dormant within
A single spark illuminates
God's enlightened path to fate
From Heaven I was sent
I am your divine complement
Our twin souls forcibly disconnected at conception
Eternities pass, impatiently waiting for direction
We intertwine only in His precise time
Hallucinating silent conversations in our minds

As time races idly by
I desire to love you with my own eyes
From Heaven two are sent
To be divine complements
Within you there is me
Without me there is no key
To unlock the galactic mystery

We collide beautifully
In a burst of cosmic energy
We love simply
From Heaven we were sent
To be divine complements
Forever and ever
Amen

# Please, Please said the Moon

Who told you to do that?
Pull the curtains back!
Lay her out
Face flat on the floor
Moans seeping
Squirming, underneath the door
Shrills escape
In constant orbit
With urgency,
I'm begging you
I want to see more

# Toe Curler

I want to make love to a song you've never sung
Oh, thief of my thoughts
I want to make love to you until I can hardly breathe as
Air spasms choke on harmony, outstanding notes

My aroma fills our nostrils and pulsates under my words
Succumb to ultimate unspoken moments of tempo
Bare fingers tap leather playfully
Throbbing to beat harder,
Softer in the name of romance
Passion rains coffee colored sweat
In cylinders filled with scratchy resonance across my chest

Seconds seem like infinity
Hooks held tightly by catchy clasps
Hours skip away as time hides
Break up wails where chants resonate deep,
Then low, bringing scorned love to concert
Shaky rhythms catch intimate grooves
Running on echo's bass,
Returning sexy pitches higher than before

Chocolate dipped fingertips
Play luxurious melodies in clandestine keys
Saturated to an unknown degree

Divided like caramel and chocolate into bitter loveliness
A blissful arc of beautiful sound

Am I, your muse?
A blindfolded music fool
Hungry like guitar strings
You are insatiable.
You ravish me
Strumming songs across my back
My nectar inebriates high off air
Shrill cries pretend to synchronize

Cloudy breaths of smoke
Trapped in purgatory
Stuck in limbo
Lyrically out of control
When your music takes hold

# C.A.N. *I watch*

You are a chocolate leg lullaby
Thick, smoky masculine thighs
Lying here next to you
Watching you sleep so peacefully
Is excruciatingly intoxicating
Shadowboxing with my sleep

I pretend to be asleep
When you nudge me
Frustrate me, with your heat
All turned around
I want
I don't want
You to touch me
Don't interrupt the voyeur in me
I am fulfilled watching you sleep

# Long Distances

If I'm here then you are there
Argue over distant planes
Why don't we cohabitate. Coincide mentally
If only for the sake of being
We are different
We—Are—Afraid
of being the same
We are not in a real place
The line is short
The distance is long
Until we go
Our separate ways.
We become happy
Separately
Beautiful solo simple
Pain is bliss
I find me
I love it
I can't trade it
Not for your happiness
I'm sorry

# Bathroom Blues

Toothpaste, toilet tissue, and old dirty magazines
Okay.

Diamond earring, gold cufflinks, and a shower with a grungy ring
Okay.

Nail polish, hairspray, and a half empty can of FDS
One single strand of over-processed red hair
Wait a minute.
Back the F'up!

Grandma was right.
Look and you shall find.
That no good man of mine!

# Once Upon A Love . . .

Once upon a magnificent love,
All I thought about was you
You and me.  Us and we
All things stunning love makes two do
Kiss, make love, intense warm embraces
Watch passion overtake your soul
Sadly, now you make me sick.
Hot words, shoot farther than hot nerves, my ears burn
Sucking in hot toxin
Love turned to hate
Love in disgrace
Disgust, tempers set aflame
I hate the taste of your name
When it rolls
Fiercely off my tongue
I spit when I think of love
I bleed my brain of lust
I'm through!

# The Ghost That Shook Me

You had to come back. Like a ghost,
From the pits of my past
You don't care
You haunt me
Taunt me

Like a well with no water
I ran out of tears
Like electricity with no outlet
I feel so dark
Like the end of a bridge
I'm over you
Our love is quiet
You made a fool of me
Two times, I'm shook

You had to come back. Like a ghost,
Sneaking out of a cryptic grave
Just when I realized
How happy I am
How happy I was
The sound of your name
Drudged up monumental pain
Like after a torrential rain
Empty promises resurfaced

Like shells on a beach
Too many to count
Like a clock that ticks
You struck out
You made a fool of me
Three times, I'm shook

Like a closed book
Like deflated expectations
Like empty promises
Like optimism moonlighting as cynicism
Like a fuse that blew
You had to leave
No explanation
I let you go in peace.

Like a petal that stretches towards the morning glow
Like a peel revealing sweet nectar
Like a proud glass of confidence
Like a rope thrown in anticipation of fire
I have hope
Let me
Just let me be in peace
Please.

# mr. opportunist

sincere is what I am
you are an opportunist
you took my heart
for no other reason
but, to tear it apart.
you don't play fair

got me some thick skin now
*balled* in a knot

# Oh, Lying Tongue

Me and my love sat on a wall
Me and my love had a big fall
Not one of our friends
None of our families
Could put me and my love back together again

Can a lie take the taste of love away
When I kiss you would it be able to heal you
Soothe the wounds I allowed to open up in you
Can a lie ever be justified?
Chalked up and charged to foolish pride
Trying to hide behind what was never true
If, I really love you.

Can a lie be forgiven with sincere promises and
Virtuous declarations and buried underneath passionate kisses
Can a lie be put on the back burner
Rekindled by fire fanned by desire and served steaming hot
Like a generous mind altering orgasm

Can a lie be taken back if on it I almost choked
When I looked in your solemn eyes
The truth escaped into the arms you held open wide
A pain this deep, a touch that cut this much
Wouldn't allow my own ears to hear

Me deceive someone that means so much
A reminder of Heaven's touch

Can a lie be set to automatically rewind
Or better yet fast forward counter clockwise
Play peek-a-boo through the view that hurt you
How would you feel if I said it hurt me more?
I hold the soul that destroyed a love
So beautiful
All that I was living for

Oh, lying tongue
What have you undone?
Can't be put back together
To begin to never tell another lie again

Me and my love sat on a wall
Me and my love had a big fall
Not one of our friends
None of our families
Could put me and my love back together again

# Cool On You

One moment in your presence feels like eternity
You are always angry about everything
The sun is shining while the moon is going down
You need to get a life
I got my whole life in front of me
I am so cool on you
I don't want to
Aint gonna consider it
Not gonna say maybe
No!

I'm not attending your pity party
A couple feet is necessary here
How about a few more
Better yet, there's the door
I am too cool on you
You are one long drawn out ass argument
I quit, I am so cool on you!

# Night Wrestler

Look at him
Fast asleep
You are not the man I once knew
I thought he was so sweet
Now I look at you bitterly
Like an octopus wrapped around me
Tentacles and holes bound me

**He won't let me escape
No air, I suffocate
Pound—Pound—Pound**
My wits depart me
You watch and laugh
He is such a fake
Snakes tie my feet
They wrestle with me tirelessly
Venom packs my veins
Air creeps like a thief, sneaking from my brain


As I rouse from outlandish dreams
Exhausted.
Dank.  And slimy.
Your arms tenderly surround me
He is still, fast asleep

I lie awake and think. For the first time at last
Tomorrow,
Best get rid of this man, that friend, those things
Tears filling my eyes. I die laughing.

# The Truth As I See It

## *About God*

## Part Three

# Empty

I feel like an empty circle
With no center.
God pencil me in
Use ink . . .
      Hurry

# *Pray Saints*

You pray and you pray and you pray
You pray and you pray and you pray
You fall on your knees
You throw up your hands
You open your mouth and shout
Lord hide me, come into my heart today
What you expect to happen, doesn't
Not on your personal time clock so to speak
You think God isn't listening
So you . . .
Doubt and you doubt and you doubt
You doubt and you doubt and you doubt
You stay on your feet
You throw your hands in your pocket
Kick bricks around
Open your mouth
Barely a whisper comes out
But this time is different, the devil sneaks in
He was waiting for his moment
And in an instant
Your life is about to begin a crazy tailspin
Get ready—Brace up
Hold on real tight
Prepare for the brawl of your life
See that speckle of an issue you prayed about

Just grew and grew, fertilized by consistent seeds of doubt

Sprouted a will of its own

Watch out!

The devil is on the move

An unnatural fiend playing foul

Throwing out all stops in frantic desperation to take your mind out

I said *watch out*!

In times of tactical warfare

Do you know what to do?

Only praying ensures you are fully prepared

Sound the alarm with your mouth

I said *watch out*!

Excuse me. Can I please have your attention?

This is not a test for the emergency send God now system

This is for real

On your knees

Assume the SOS position

I said *watch out*!

Watch out!

Pray—Pray

Pray the devil out of the tangled weave of destruction going on inside your head

So what if Satan is on a mission

You have been conditioned to beat his evil system

So what, it only seems like an uphill battle, facing disaster

And Satan has an unfair supernatural advantage

I said *pray*

Jesus is on the way

Hold out till He gets here
I said *pray*
An eternity isn't too late
The souls of your descendents are at stake
With a new sense of urgency
Jesus will come through
Believe that He heard you
He is all the strength you need
His promise to you
You need to pray—saints
Fall on your knees
Throw up your hands
Open your mouth
An army of *angels* will fall out
And stomp the devil out

# Perfect

Perfect house.
Perfect car.
Perfect job.
Perfect husband.
Perfect wife.
Perfect child.
Perfect life.
I don't think so.
Superficial perfect illusions mask worldly trouble.

Perfect peace surpasses all understanding.
Perfect abundance in all things you touch.
Perfect joy in your heart.
Perfect mercy forgives every sin.
Perfect love makes life worth living.
Perfect choice
Perfect God.

# Deuteronomy

(*the words* Moses *spoke to all* Israel)


little one, hear me for sure,
Deuteronomy 1:39
children who do not know good from bad;
they will enter the land, and take possession of it

oh, what have we left them
this?
cursed earth
tangled and mangled
we cursed them from birth
branded our past hurts
scorched their hearts with fire
young eyes old weary and tired
like a torch in the dark
we made them easy marks
watch them!

where do they go
moaning and stinking
down a timeless road
everything, we pillaged and raped it
like damned vagrants
a once insignificant light

is worth more than a man
He put down His hand
God must have had all He could stand
when does it end

Exodus 20 and 5 says
not for another four generations
peace.

# Some Things Take Time

It has taken a long time to get comfortable
In this skin, with this past, shaking my mistakes
Mixing a sour twist with sugary sense
Into a cocktail of success where I, *win.*

It has taken a long time to understand
I own my dreams; Destiny is reality churning on a crooked,
Jagged path. Although hard to pursue,
I take ownership of those too.

It has taken a long time to stand against
The trampled hopes of my mother,
The immense anger of my father.
Shielding my eyes from despair dripping from my siblings,
Afraid to look less my light flicker and grow dimmer
Savoring the bitterness of my inheritance, gifted,
This ruptured soul which proved more blessing than curse
Wisdom knows the secret that has made me whole.

It has taken a long time to grasp
I can give all my love away, reserve a little for myself and
Somehow there remains an abundance to start all over again
My love recycles and squares into an infinite gift attaining more
Energy than the entire world's carbon footprint.

It has taken a long time to learn the value
Woe is me, of self sacrifice,
If I bestow more than I've been given,
The opportunity to shift the future appears,
Eradicate my yesterday, and give positively to eternity
Possess my self-fulfilling prophecy,
My son, my seed will go farther than me
The time is now to be accountable to my dynasty
Make haste as there is very little time to waste. *Run Son. Run.*

It has taken a long time to trust
In the true value of friends, I am not the Crowning Judge to
Preside over the true hearts of men
Outstretched hands only appear to be demanding,
Though I frantically push away,
They pull me back, gently embracing me,
They are family.

It has taken a long time to learn
The weightlessness of forgiveness
A most intricate act to master, all other lessons seem irrelevant
The transparent deed nobody else can see
Lingers stealthily underneath a mirrored mask
A reflection of lies and deception
Only to be broken by the loving Hands of Acceptance.

# The Truth

*Sheket*!
The truth can't be quieted.
The nature of man, when they hear it,
Instinct says to silence it.
The truth comes forth anyway
Truth can't be halted.
Truth is happiness.
Truth hopes
Truth hurts
Truth heals
Hallelujah truth!
From out of the Word is spews
Into the world it moves
Man into the realm of eternal love, peace, and joy.

*Sheket – Hebrew for quiet*

# Acknowledge Me

Sister,
What's wrong?
Pride snatched words from your tongue?
Your neck won't twirk to work enough too simply—nod
You see me
I smiled at you,
Made room for you on the pew
We met eye to eye
Me and you.
I must by hook or by crook become invisible
You gave me a silent humph
I gave my full attention
I refuse to succumb, become numb, and act dumb
I'll wait.  Your mama taught you better manners than that—I hope
If not, it's never too late. Learn on your own
O, you're too glammed up and made up to pay me any mind
I see.  Sister, relax,
Unfurl your mask
Open up your lips
Smiling won't crack your Mac
I promise, try
I have on some too
My favorite shade, c-thru
Are you worried about anonymity?
I am here seeking God
I am your sister—In Christ
Now.  Now, don't cry

We have someone very special in common
We are the same sister,
Show your beautiful teeth
Open your mouth and let your smile run free
Release yourself and acknowledge me

Brother, why?
You don't have to be interested
To say hi
Neither am I
Is this what we do?
Forever walk in circles,
Like two mute fools
Eyes intense on an invisible prize beyond
Me looking at you *and*
You pretending not to see this giant tree
I am not your enemy
This treatment deserves to be out in the streets
Insanity, I will take no part
Today is the day for new starts
This is not the behavior of Christ
Jesus spoke
Jesus healed
Jesus led
Jesus fed
A multitude of strangers
In the Good Book
The Samaritan female, at the well,
She ran back to tell
About the man from distant lands

He spoke volumes to her heart
Not one disciple had the audacity
To question her chastity
I nodded at you
Looked you right in the eye
Gave you the respect you were due
What you did in turn—not cool
I opened my mouth to speak
You gave me the once over,
Turned your shoulder
Is this the way a *king* greets a passing *queen*?
Next time you're in the presence of greatness
God's wonderfully made creation
Remember your obligation
Take sex out of the equation
Greet me with no hesitation
Show your beautiful teeth
Open your mouth and let your smile run free
Release yourself and acknowledge me

Parents teach your children in the way of the word
Train a child in the way he should go,
And when she is old he will not turn
Release your seed, a new beginning seek
They too,
Should take the time to—acknowledge me

# Closer

One step closer to Him
My sweet redeemer
How Heavenly, my imagination roams
I can feel Him drawing me home
A simple dreamer
Fast asleep with open eyes
My heart navigates through loving chambers
I can't wait, my excitement elevates
An uncalculated pace
Behold blind faith
He commands a time that doesn't exist
Reality ceases in the wrinkles of my dreams
No fear where fear should dwell
Words give no value to this priceless moment
I am quiet

Peace surrounds and I can see it
Sheer, opalescent tears break through
I am magnetically drawn to You
Loving upon a magnificent Being
I am on the edge
Lord don't release me
Hold me nearer
I can feel Your mercy

I deserve You
A wonderful and forgiving truth
Oh, my Savior
I have never felt so close to You

# The Lion

I long to lie at His feet
I place my tender heart in capable hands
I long to lay in His arms
I am impatiently anticipating that day
I am seeking Him
He orders the trees to whisper my name
I am seeking peace
Calling me through the fog of my imperfections
Dew trickles onto my face
Until I become a waterfall of tears
Oh, wounded heart can you feel
My spirit is disturbed
*Time* to face the Lion in the Midst

Look up
Meek and holy
Mighty and full of honor
Majestic and honest
A blinding light of truth!
Yet I see clearly, as never before
There's a Lion in the Midst

No, I am ashamed
Fall to my knees, humble
The Lion caresses me

Forgiveness rips and shreds my soul
No longer searching for joy,
The Lion has made me whole

# Our Love

You distract me with your masculinity
Draw me in with your femininity
Protecting and nurturing
You place an absurd fear in me
A wrath so terrifying
Don't laugh at me Lord
I experience pain in reverse when you are near
Guilt riddles my actions
Yet, you love me still
My heart beats, hurts, and bursts for you Lord.
Invisible music makes me skip til I'm dizzy
You're my sweet cavity
Tasty prayers bound my lips
We are a part of the trinity
The Holy Divinity takes over me
I like it. Can you do it again?
Don't laugh at me Lord
We were destined to meet
Thank you for waiting for me.

# This Morning I Know

Are you telling me?
When I thought there was only despair and pain
No hope for the shape I was in
I only had to call on Jesus and he would be my friend!

Are you telling me?
When all else fails,
A word of prayer will prevail!

Are you telling me?
All my needs will be met
All I have to do is give him the utmost respect!

Are you telling me?
All my enemies will be defeated,
All I have to do is read the word
Believe it and mean it!

Are you telling me?
Everything I've ever done is erased,
It doesn't matter anymore except in this place!

Are you telling me?
God is my provision and more

I only need to speak my name on the roll,
What have I been waiting for!

Are you telling me?
I can start all over,
Tell the devil to move over!
In Christ all things are created new!
Including me too!
Thank God I know now!

# The Truth As I See It
## *About Life*

## Part Four

# A Social Butterfly is Alive

I'm sitting here thinking. I am thinking and trying really hard to remember the day I was born. No, not the day my mother gave birth to me, of course I know that. I am bringing to recollection the day God first whispered in my ear, "You shall live and not die."

*Numbers 4:19 So that they may live and not die when they come near the most holy things, do this for them: Aaron and his sons are to go into the sanctuary and assign to each man his work and what he is to carry.*

The entire day felt like a set-up, the day I was born for the second time. I went about my miserable life as usual, nothing stood out. I yelled at my son, went to work, and came home yelling at the dog. Frustration leaked out of my pores and followed me around like a thief pilfering joy. To be honest, I didn't think I deserved joy, so a thief could easily steal what I didn't think I owned without me noticing. What was it to me? There were no signs and no flashing neon lights warning me that my life was about to change forever, for the better.

*Deuteronomy 16:15 For the LORD your God will bless you in all your harvest and in all the work of your hands and your joy will be complete.*

I slid into my seat. I was late and damp from the evening's downpour which almost became my excuse to turn right around and head home. There was something about the music, the lights, and the ambiance that night. I decided to stay for a little while. I lifted my hands, and let the aura in the room soothe me. The raging war inside me began to settle as I nestled into the comfort of the Lord's presence. I raised my arms higher, towards Heaven. I wanted God to snatch me up; I needed him to rescue me—immediately. Two friends found me and my defeated spirit was surrounded on all sides by His presence.  He knew exactly what I needed; there was nowhere to run.

*Psalm 31:5 Restore to me the joy of your salvation and grant me a willing spirit, to sustain me.*

That night, as I grasped my friend's hand and prayed obediently over her life and she over mine, I let go. For the first time ever, I didn't think about myself. I didn't sneak in a prayer for myself as I prayed for blessings, overflow, and peace in her life. I put me on hold and let go of all the pain, lies, hurt, and ails that I had ever felt. He knew what he was doing. He forced me to drop it right there, as there was no way I could hold God's hand, all my baggage, and pray for someone else too.

*Job 42:10 After Job had prayed for his friends, the Lord made him prosperous again and gave him twice as much as he had before.*

No, it wasn't an instantaneous happening, two winks from a genie and, "bam, problems be gone!" It was more of a peaceful surrender. He proved to me that He was God. He alone, from then on would be handling my cares. I became free to move about my life, to love, and to live on purpose. I climbed out of my dark hole of despair, my cocoon, and shook the dust from my wings. Of course it gets a little unsteady sometimes, but finally, A Social Butterfly is Alive.

*Psalm 18:2 The Lord is my rock, my fortress and my deliverer; my God is my rock, in whom I take refuge. He is my shield and the horn of my salvation, my stronghold.*

# *It's Independence Day!*
# *Personalized*

Today, I too, celebrate My Personal Independence.

I have my own declarations on which I stand. There are so many distractions and personal battles that become dream killers and steal time if left unharnessed. Of those we must become independent. To become independent of a thing, you must have a revolution. America did it. The Thirteen Colonies stood against the Parliament of Great Britain and won. Sometimes, you have to go to war with yourself. Pull out the gloves, the pen, go in the closet, drive along the coast, jog, or whatever it is you must do to make space for your personal revolution. Go in swinging, chop down  defeat, and come out victorious. Begin living with a new vengeance. It's amazing what one can accomplish once aligned and focused.

**I'd like to share my personal revolutionary platform**:
1. Me - Love me. Be my most honest supporter, advocate, critic, and cheerleader
2. Purpose - Find it. Find it. Find it. It will make you happy, I promise
3. Procrastination - No more Talking about it or complaining about it. Be about it
4. Doubt - Do, despite doubt til there is no doubt
5. Fear - Do, despite fear til you are not afraid

6. Pride - Get rid of it before self destruction (Proverbs 16:18). *I know this one is hard*

7. God - Actually He comes first, listed last here as He makes it possible to do all of the above

Happy Personal Independence Day!

# What's Your Default Setting?

We are more like computers than we realize. Think about the day you brought your brand new cutting edge computer home. Oh, how you eagerly ripped open the cardboard, popped a couple bubbles on the bubble wrap, and finally the Hachi Tachi 3000 was in your trembling hands! What a beauty. Clean, with no scratches or blemishes from the top to the bottom. I can just see you now, plugging it into the outlet while listening for the electrical currents to signal the first signs of life. On to the installation process; if you are anything like me and not a computer programmer, you opted for the standard default settings because Mom suggested it.

Let's fast forward to when the brand new smell was only a distant memory. You've become an expert at running your machine. Everything worked as it should, but inside you wished it would do a little more of what you specifically needed. Once you really had the swing of it, you began to have some expectations. The more you grew the less functionality you seemed to get out of it. Everybody in your family had the same exact laptop. But, yours just didn't work for you anymore, wreaking havoc on your life. It's time to go back to those default settings Mom suggested and tweak them. It's time to tweak you.

We were all born with default settings; genetics, and principles. Your father has brown eyes and you have brown eyes. Your mother was a Christian therefore, you are a Christian. Your sister went to a prestigious college, but you couldn't pass Algebra to save your life. Your cousin is a mad scientist, but you hate CSI. Your son is a gladiator on the football field, but you prefer to read a suspenseful novel on a Monday night. You stress over feeling different from everyone else around you. You judge yourself from their eyes and by what you *think* their standards should be and feel inadequate. Why?

Interests are only add-ons, my friend. An add-on is something you don't have to have. An add-on is not a requirement to a happy life; it's an interest that you find interesting. Defining yourself by someone else's interests is such a waste of time. So, if you don't have any time to waste—then don't. Be productive with the little time you have left at the end of the day. Focus on your interests and add purpose to your life.

Don't make failure your default setting because you are trying to walk in someone else's size seven shoes that you can't squeeze your eight in to save your life. You wear a size eight and that person wears a size seven. It's neither a good nor a bad thing. It's just a thing. Spend that wasted time squeezing purpose inside *your* mind. Figure out what works for you and go do that!

My grandmother used to tell us (her kids and grandkids) all the time, "Don't set out any shade trees for me to sit under." I was an adult before I really understood what she meant. Don't let anyone else write out a plan for your life and expect you to adhere to it. Do your own thing! Every attempt you make to be me will make you miserable unless whatever I am doing is in your plan. Don't even consider my add-ons unless it will add value to what you have going. Even then, tweak the plan to make it work for you.

You are your own person. Be you. You have your own dreams. Dream them. You have your own interests. Pursue them. You have your own life, live it.

# Aspire

By the time my words meet reality
You are already a man to be
Great king in the making
I have given you all of me
Merely a woman
Pouring until there is nothing
Into a vessel of opportunity
Hop up on my shoulders
Run into chance
Aspire high. Stand tall
You are a Man.
When you doubt what to do
Know Mom will pray
But, you should too
And, let God guide you.

# The Trials of Raising a Man
# The Lesson

Raising my son is the most beautiful, arduous task I have ever had the pleasure of performing. So many times I've wanted to give up because I wasn't getting my way, or better yet, my desired result. Yet, who would be there to build him up the way only a mother can. I still get so confused over exactly the right thing to do. I refer to the vision of what I think a man is and build towards that. I am very proud to say, that to date I have a great son. I mean, if I don't think he's great, who else would? More importantly, would he?

Every day I watch him grow just a little bit more. He ventures a little bit farther away. *It won't be long now,* I think to myself. He no longer holds on to my belt loop. Every once in a while he looks over his shoulder for Mommy's approval. Whew, that was close. My baby, my son, my man child, he still needs me. I hug myself gently, but sooner than I care to imagine, I will be all I have. We are both preparing for the parting. I do not want him to be so attached that he would want to stay. I believe that a man must know how to make his own way in this world. There are no exceptions or excuses allowed for men. My job is to make him strong enough to go.

He is changing so fast, I race to keep up. Allowing him to change begins with me. I've begun with the way I talk to him and the way I treat him. I must be mindful at all times of his self-esteem. I need to be aware of where his dreams may take him. I look at myself and make changes because it's important how he views me, *the first lady of his life*. Am I the woman I want him to bring home to me? The man he becomes will determine the woman he shares his life with. That is one of the many things I find myself thinking about frequently.

Sometimes, when we clown around, I feel his strength. His physical power is growing. Yes, he notices and is amazed at himself. Wait, I need you to slow down my son. I see you've grown taller than me and yes, you are developing quickly; however, please do not forget I am the boss. I seem to remind him more often of boundaries than ever before. I am your mother; your sole provider and somewhere way down the line, your friend. To me, it's like mixing business with pleasure, and once you cross the line, it's hell getting your professionalism back. Of course spankings and frequent chastising are out of the question at this point. My boy is huge. I win only when I challenge his mind to think reasonably or when I appeal to his sensitive side.

More explanations are necessary, but I'm glad he trusts me enough to ask me. I have moved a long way from talking to him to conversing with him; even children have something to say. My favorite times with my son are easy conversations during rush hour. I love to be locked in the car, just the two of us—talking. He is pretty handy in the kitchen, so preparing and eating dinner together is always nice. I have learned so much about him, about who he is becoming and what he would like to be. My son is hilarious and he always says his quick wit came from me. You know what, sharing who Mom is as a real person with goals and dreams independent of him has done wonders for our relationship. More God is imperative now, more than ever. I encourage him to pray for himself because he won't be able to fly over life's obstacles on the wings of Mommy's prayers.

There are lessons I have to repeat like a broken record. I allow him to misplace them in his busy mind. Just like me in my youth, he will remember later. Aren't those little jewels to live by from Grandma more precious, more meaningful today than when you were a child? The right words come back just when you need them most. My son will be no exception. He will learn to recall the sound of my voice when he needs to hear it the most.

- Know God for yourself, one day you will have to cover your own family!
- Mom is in charge—period.
- When I say *failure,* he finishes with *is not an option.* Exactly and don't forget it.
- You are a leader; you might as well get used to it and start now unless you like being lead.
- Be gentle with little kids, you were once that small.
- Be a friend to the friendless, we all share this future.
- Men shouldn't put people down or gossip. It's a sign of weakness and insecurity. Do you know who you are? Well, that's all that matters, worry about you.
- Did you hear the instructions or do you like running around in circles?

- Are we a team or two separate entities? Let's get on the same page.
- You are smart. You are beautiful and if you believe it so will everyone else.
- What do you want to do with your life? Well, go do it!
- If you don't practice or prepare, you will fail. Is that the result you want?
- I know you don't have your own Dad in your life. It should be that much more important that you be what you never had (and not just for your biological children). Especially, since you know what it feels like.
- Everything I am not, you can be. *Here*, take Mom's mistakes as your head start.
- Don't lie, it opens the door to theft, murder, cheating, etc., none of which are Mommy supported activities.
- Don't just say okay. What is your opinion? Have one and stand on it.
- Pay attention to what is going on around you; it's not all about you all the time.
- I don't want to hear any excuses or complaints unless you need my opinion and have thought about a resolution.
- Who said no again? Who the hell is that?
- In life you get what you deserve. Do you think you deserve this, be it good or bad?
- Character is hard to repair once flawed publicly, even at home. Always be aware of your persona.
- Never give Mom a gift that is not wrapped (his wife will appreciate that).

- Stand on my shoulders and not by my side.
- Sometimes Mom has it *all* wrong. Please accept my apology. I am a woman trying to raise—a great man.
- As I interpret the Bible to say, train up a child in the way he should go. Isn't he already a child? Hasn't he mastered being a child? Therefore, aren't my instructions to train him *up* to be a man? At least I'm trying the best I can as a woman!

I love my beautiful son.

# The Trials of Raising a Man
# The Lost Village

The village is being pillaged
We laugh from righteous, sanctified perches
Holy art thou?
Generations march idly by
Lost
Robbed in hindsight
The village is now empty

I remember being about thirteen years old. I had the audacity to put one leg over the other in an attempt to cross them in church. I paid no attention to the fact that my skirt rose up above my knees. I was young or maybe I didn't care. But, she did. A mother of the church walked quickly towards me with a look of contempt on her face, shaking out a white hanky with a white laced edge until it snapped loudly, breaking the air with its crispness.

"Fast tailed girl!" she hissed, placing the hanky over my knees in an effort to conceal my goodies. She walked away rolling her eyes at the audacity of my brazenness.

She was not having it, not in her church and not on her watch. She marched right over to my grandmother and whispered in her ear. I watched them, feeling nervous as they whispered while glancing in my direction. The frown on Grandma's face needed no words. I knew what was going to happen on the way home. I adjusted the

hanky on my knees and waited in uneasy anticipation of what was to
come as a result of embarrassing Grandma at village headquarters—
church. The family, the church, the neighborhood, the school, and
the corner market were all parts of the village.

As of late, society has officially lost that *one village* feeling. The
village is missing in massive proportions. Why? Do we no longer
need a village to raise a child?

Why are we afraid to talk to the children of our dear friends if
we catch them misbehaving outside of their parents watchful eyes?
Why do we not snatch the pants up of Young Junior and tell him to
go put on a belt! Or explain to Little Miss Fast Tail privately how
to come before the Lord instead of whispering and pointing at her
from almighty sanctified perches. "That's a shame, tsk, tsk, tsk."
Yes, it is a shame, but if you're not going to help then you've lost
your right to gossip. That little boy in despair, most likely doesn't
have a man around. God said for us to allow the fatherless to eat
and be satisfied by the works of our hands and He will bless us
(Deuteronomy 14:29). He was talking about you and me. You are
the village; I am the village. We are all accountable to the children
under our watchful eyes.

In lieu of togetherness, we are now afraid. Yes, fear is both
missing and present in massive abundance. We live in it, then hide
because of it, and get behind it. We live in fear that the wrong
somebody is going to tell our child what to do. Sometimes, fear can
be valid. However, you have to trust someone. Why not start with
your immediate village? Your neighbor is home when you are away
and can let you know or shut down what is really going on while
the cat's away. I don't mind telling the neighborhood boys to go

put on shoes, no fighting, or to pick up their trash left in my yard. My guard rises quickly if I suspect any suspicious activity in my neighborhood. I care about their safety. They are my boys too!

We don't want our children to fear us; let alone their teacher. If our children don't like their 5th grade teacher, we go off on the teacher. The entire time we bury our insecurity by hiding the reality that our child is also hard to handle at home. Instead we should instill dread in him of coming home after a long day of acting up in school. We must work with other figures of authority and not against them. When children realize adults are working together, and what you do in the streets will follow them home, they really think twice about misbehaving. My child does not fear me, but he is afraid of the consequences of unacceptable behavior. In the beginning; *Adam and Eve were in the garden and scurried to cover themselves when they heard the voice of the Lord drawing near.* Why do you think two adults ran and hid from our loving Lord and Savior? It is simple, Adam and Eve were afraid of the consequences of disobeying the Supreme Authority Figure (Genesis 3:10).

We live in fear that somebody (whoever that is) will think we are a bad parent. Even parents need a village a, "what can I do with this child," consortium to bounce ideas and exchange strategies with. Don't be ashamed to reach out. I remember once bawling at the altar and a good friend wrapped her arms around me in comfort. I later told her about the issue I was having with my son. Since she had three great adult kids, I figured she would be a great resource having been there and done it all. She *snatched* my son up and through clenched teeth gave him an earful of sound advice. In embarrassment, he began to cry. Somehow, another concerned person talking to him actually helped the situation. She hugged and kissed him and told him she loved him. She prayed with both of us. No, it didn't hurt me one bit to have someone outside of my family chastise my child. I trust and respect her. Even as an adult and a mom, I still need chastising whenever necessary.

Today as I look back on all of the public displays of chastisement, I endured, I am grateful. All of them shaped who I am today. I am grateful for every single experience, for every finger that ever wagged disapprovingly in my face. I am grateful for every time I heard the words fast *tailed girl* while I was told to *go put on a slip!*

It is time for all of us to understand that accepting assistance doesn't mean that you are giving up. If this were a democracy the village would be the Senate and make up Congress. I would be the President. If governing parties work against each other, nothing gets accomplished. I have a huge job on my hands and I need my village. I need help, guidance, and support on those dark days when I've exhausted all other avenues. When I can't think of anything else to do you my village, give me the extra fuel to keep trying. Thank you for being my cheerleader, coach, and especially mediator. It's not like my son came with a manual or something. What do I know about Raising a Man?

It is true that my son needs me. He also needs your eyes in the back of my head to catch what I've missed. Although the village went out of style like neighborhood watch and block parties, can I ask a favor of you? If you ever see my son out in the big, wide, world acting up, just give him the eye or an earful and call me. If we work together, we will make a *man out of that boy*!

# The Trials of Raising a Man Excuse me. Mine is missing the manual

*How hard could this b*e? I wondered to myself as I looked at the beautiful new baby snuggled sweetly in my arms. It had only been a few moments since we welcomed him into the world from right underneath my heart. The doctor placed him in my hands. God placed him in my care. Just that fast, I loved him and was already thinking about what was best for him. Raising my son was going to be a piece of cake. *Or so I thought.*

Clothes on his back. Check.
Feed him. Check.
Send him to school. Check.

At 18, off on his own, he will go into the world to be the man God called him to be. Right? Uh, wrong! There is so much more to parenthood than necessities. There is so much work to do between birth and the magical age of adulthood, eighteen years old. There are smiles, frowns, heartaches, struggles, successes, failures, and triumphs! Parenthood, for sure has taught me (the hard way) there is more to life than me and what I want.

To begin, I don't remember having so many distractions like the internet, a cell phone, an IPod, or a television at my disposal with 200 channels to flip idly through. I never had my very own Mommy at my complete disposal either. I rush around picking him up, dropping him off, and arranging every detail of his life. Why in the world did I honestly think I could get *him* to think and make good choices? I made all the decisions and told him what to think about them. He had it made with life at his disposal. Shoes too big for a kid. Hello, Mom! Everything is not supposed to be for him, but for his benefit! So he can grow as a man.

It took me a long time to understand that my son was his own person. No matter how much I wanted to see him walk down the right path, I couldn't force it on him, nor do it for him, or bribe him the entire way. My son has a mind of his own. I only have total control over my reactions and never his actions. Because of that, I introduced accountability into our household. For every action, I gave him a set of standard of reactions. A=B, always, and without exceptions. If A was a positive action then B was a positive reaction, and vice versa. I cannot begin to tell you how much that freed me. I no longer had to bear the burden of punishing him. He knew the consequences; he punished himself and it had nothing to do with me. Can you say sigh of relief?

There are times I may have made a mountain out of a molehill. At the time, did I know it was a molehill? The two can get very confusing when it's all unknown terrain and you don't have a handy dandy manual in your pocket.

All I know is that I wanted my child to be perfect. I want him to be successful. I want him to be a great mountain of a man one day. So, I pushed him. I pushed him just as hard as I push myself. When he failed to meet the expectations that I never fully discussed and agreed upon with him, I felt as though I failed too. I took it personally and we both crashed. I have since learned that I can revel in his successes with him. I can hold his hand and comfort him when he fails. That is all Mommy can do. A man must learn how to deal with failure on his own. Now we talk about what made him succeed in a particular endeavor, so he will know what works. We talk about what made him fail a particular endeavor, so he will know what doesn't work. We talk about everything. The doors to communication are now open.

Knowing and accepting that I cannot live my son's life for him helps me the most during the trials I face—trying to raise a man. I cannot do everything for him. I cannot think for him or he will never be able to think for himself. Giving him the answer is so much easier and less time consuming for me than guiding him to find it on his own. However, it is my job to think long term as to what is best for him. If I do not teach him the survival skills necessary to live in a changing world, for sure he will fail. Mommy will not always be there to fix his boo-boo. I better teach him today how to apply a Band-Aid and run despite pain. This world will not love him as much as I do. The world won't hold him close and become excited over his heartbeat everyday. He must learn to look to me for comfort and look towards the world when it's time to conquer. He must learn how to fail and try again until he succeeds. He must learn to trust his own judgment and lean on God with all he believes.

Yes, my son is really a fantastic kid! I am humbled to be his Mom. I thank God for choosing me to be his guide on this journey called life. I am enjoying my role so much more now that we have finally figured this mother and son thing out.

# I Hope Your Ear Falls Off

I remember sitting in church one Sunday about ten years ago. I don't remember the sermon topic or the scripture. The pastor decided to share a personal event about his past with the congregation. It was so quiet in the sanctuary that you could hear a needle fall on a bed of hay. It was a miracle indeed that not one baby whimpered as the pastor became transparent right before our very eyes in hopes of turning a light on for us. We were all holding our breath. Smack dab in the middle of telling his story, he stopped.

He said "Now I'm trying to help somebody overcome this situation right now. But, I can see y'all can't wait to get home and run your mouth about what I'm about to tell you. But if you do, I hope your ear falls off." He then delved back into the story he was sharing which I don't even remember, but his statement has stuck with me all of these years.

Whenever I think about that day with my new grown woman eyes, I can see clearly what he saw. Have you ever watched two or more people gossip? There is an intense look of interest on their faces. It is like a static string of electricity connects and freezes them together. One person's lips will move, while the listeners are held engrossed and captivated in utter silence lest they miss the single tangible string of sustenance seeping into their ear. My pastor saw this picture that day long ago as he stood before the congregation offering his testimony in hopes of touching one soul in the name of the Lord.

Gossip, whether intended or not, has a most hurtful effect on all parties involved. In the midst of having a discussion about someone, you have to stop and ask yourself if what you are saying may cause dissention. I don't know about you, but there were times that I learned more than I wanted or needed to know about someone else through gossip. After knowing what didn't concern me, I was forever changed. I began to look at that person differently than had I not known. I liken it to Eve and the apple. I'm sure it looked pretty interesting and the lies of the serpent seemed pretty tasty going down her ear canal. Look at the world now, we got greedy for secrets and lost the Garden of Eden.

Are you talking about solutions or people? That is the key to healthy conversations regarding people that are not present to represent themselves. It is one thing to call your friends to say, "May's house burned down, can you help with food, shelter, or clothing?" It is another to call your friends to say, "This is between you and me, but May burned her house down because she found her husband in bed with another woman and she set them both on fire. I'm not going to do anything for her; I don't know why she called me anyway." May called because she thought she had trusted friends. If there is nothing I am willing to do. or nothing *I can do,* then I should probably find something else to talk about, as I just took myself out of the equation. I'm sure gossipers can find enough of their own business to talk about to keep their tongues busy for the rest of their lives.

On the other hand, we all have to learn to be quiet. I have found that by doing more listening than talking I can figure out rather quickly who I can and can't trust. Of course I learned the hard way, but like grandma says, "Bought sense is better than none." I can't be so naive to think I do not share in the process of my business being spread thinly through the streets. If you feed a gossip, he will be loyal until you have nothing interesting to give him. Only by being silent can you protect yourself.

Even if you have already invested hours, months, years, or a lifetime gossiping about others, it is never too late to just stop before *your ear falls off.*

*Proverbs 26: 20-21 Without wood a fire goes out; without gossip a quarrel dies down. As charcoal to embers and as wood to fire, so is a quarrelsome man for kindling strife.*

# *Using Adversity,*
# *To Get There*

Adversity has the capability to bring out skills in us we don't recognize or appreciate. Probably because we are so focused on just plain ole surviving; never imagining *I* can have more. I'm not saying the prosperous don't ever live in a funk of complacency and contentment.

Your grandparents received the gold pen after 50 years with the same company. *You want more.* They dedicated themselves to the same job until retirement. *You can't.* You can still hear her authoritative voice in your head when you contemplated starting your own business, "Baby, you better keep that good job." *You want something more meaningful to you.* I bet Grandma's skin never experienced the soft, luxurious fabric of the sofa hiding underneath the protective covering, did it? *You feel it, don't you? You long for it.*

Indulge yourself in the plush pillows of your imagination and figure this thing out! You have already been focused on surviving! Get to striving! Claim what's on the other side of adversity. Do you know what it is? Prosperity! Couple your survival skills with your purpose and become unstoppable. What do you have to lose if you didn't have anything to start with?

# Excerpt:

## *Running from Solace*

## Coming 2010

Once, she flung a heavy ashtray at my head. Blood spewed onto my new, pink dress like red polka dots because I didn't hear her calling me, "Naomi! Naomi!" I was trying frantically to reach her special ashtray from underneath the bed, so I didn't hear her the first time. I could tell she was getting mad, but I almost had it in my hand when I heard her say, "If I call you one more time!" That did it for me; I knew I was getting a whooping.

"Don't make me call you again, Naomi!" Mama said again as I presented her with what she was impatiently waiting on. She went crazy on me, hitting me on the top of my head over and over again with the ashtray.

"You ungrateful little bitch!" she yelled repeatedly in my face. I tried to cover my head with my arms, until they grew tired and I gave up. Fury danced in her eyes and spit sprinkled over me like morning mist. My eyes burned from the tiny flecks of ashes that fell from the ashtray. I tried closing them tightly; still warm blood trickled slowly down my forehead. It penetrated my eyelids and cooled the burning sensation.

"Yeah, you must like gettin hit!" Mama screamed so loud I wanted my ears to close. I preferred the times when she whooped me and she was silent. Out of sheer luck, at some point during the beating, I passed out. I usually did.

When I woke up, I was lying on my bed, which almost never had any sheets. I was still wearing what was left of my tattered dress. It was covered in dried blood, more red than pink now. I didn't have the urge go look in the mirror. I knew already, since this was not the first time. My eyes would be really fat, and this time, one was closed, I couldn't open it. The other only opened partially. I was able to peek out of it. Raised, sweltering, purplish bruises would cover my arms, back and face—the usual damage. My head throbbed. I couldn't lift my arms. I was afraid to move anyway, afraid to breathe. I laid there as still as I could. I followed the dingy, white, lace hem of what was once my pretty dress down from my knee to my ankle and across the dirty mattress, as it fell off the bed onto the floor where I could see it no more. I wanted to cry, but no tears came. *I must have run out of tears,* I thought to myself as I managed a painful smile that made my head ache from the inside out even more.

"Nobody likes ole crybaby, bad assed kids! Shut. The. Fuck Up!" Mama hated it when I cried; she always said I only wanted people to feel sorry for me. So, if I had run out of tears that would've made my Mama very happy. I would never have to hear her call me a crybaby anymore and maybe she will smile at me like she does when I light her cigarettes on the stove. Well, not like the time when I lit the skinny white one on both ends. I shivered a little when I thought of the whooping I got for doing that. How was I supposed to know, when it didn't have the brown paper on one end of it? She'd always taught me to light the white end only. Ever since that time, I always ask first, "Which end, Mommy?" I didn't want to disappoint her again or make her mad.

I had an urge to go pee. I was comfortable and warm. I didn't want to move, plus that's when the pain would start. Of course my head hurt and I had some aches all over my body, but as long as I kept really still it wasn't that bad. It could have been worse, like some of the other times before. Moving would be impossible and I knew it, so I didn't.

More than the pain, more than anything else, I didn't want Mama to wake up. She was lying right behind me. Her arm was gently positioned around my waist. Her hand rested on my stomach. I was balled in a knot with my back touching her stomach. I knew she was still asleep. I could feel her breath blowing softly on the back of my neck. It actually felt nice. Every few minutes or so, I could hear her teeth grinding against each other or her jaw making a popping sound. The noises terrified me. Still, this is when I loved her the most and felt the safest, when Mama was laying next to me—asleep. I didn't have the nerve to wake her up just to go pee. So, I just lay there quietly and watched the lace through one eye as I listened to her breathe peacefully until I fell asleep.

I went in and out of sleep, waking up almost every time I felt Mama move. Mama nudged me awake with kisses. Her juicy lips left wet marks on my cheeks. I opened my eye slowly and Mama gasped, as I turned towards her. Then she smiled, "Hey Mama's baby," she cooed.

"Hi, Mama," I said drowsily.

I felt the dampness on my back as I slowly came out of my sleep. I started wondering how long Mama had been up. *Did she know? Did it get on her?* So many thoughts raced through my mind. I didn't know what to do, so I pretended to be terribly exhausted as she kissed me and explained what I needed to do so she wouldn't have to whoop me anymore. Sometimes I needed to be a good girl and do exactly as she says, "It's not good for little girls not to listen to their mothers," she said with tears in her eyes.

"Yes, Mama," was all I could answer over and over again after every statement she made. I just wanted her to go away. It hurt too much to nod my head or move my lips for that matter, "I promise. I will be a good girl, from now on," I attempted my most forgiving look, despite the pain it caused to move my face. That's what she was waiting for anyway, for me to show some semblance of forgiveness so she could be okay. I agreed that I was wrong. *Just go please,* I kept thinking.

"I love you baby," she said as she reached towards me.

I flinched in anticipation thinking maybe she saw it, felt it. She saw me flinch and then she snatched back her hand. I closed my eye quickly in preparation of her smack across my face. Mama hated it when I flinched. The hit took too long to come, so I peeked through my eye again. She was already walking out the door closing it softly behind her. "I love you too Mama," I said to the empty room.

I had to get up and get changed before she came back. I remember willing my aching little body to move. I was so tired, but Mama hated when I peed in the little bed we shared. There were already so many old stains on the smelly mattress and just as many spankings for doing it. No sooner than I raised myself up off of the bed, I heard the door open. I didn't turn around. I stared at the dust around the window sill over the bed. The lace from my dress dangled and tickled my knee as I stood there imagining myself invisible.

"Naomi. Baby, did you pee yourself?" she didn't sound mad. I didn't say anything, taking a moment to decide whether I should tell the truth or not. "MiMi?" she waited. Okay, she wasn't mad or maybe she was trying to trick me. The only time she ever called me MiMi was when she was in a good mood.

"I . . . I'm sorry," I stammered.

"I peed when I was . . . when I was sleep." I said without turning around. I lowered my head and looked for the wet spot on the mattress with my one open eye. My wet underwear suddenly felt colder. The air hitting my damp back sent a chill over me and I shivered or maybe it was the impending beating that I knew was coming. I still didn't move, not even when I heard her sigh loudly. The pain all over my body began to come alive and my aches began to scream. I continued to stare at the window sill; the dust seemed so interesting. If I stared really hard I could see shapes. There's an N, like the N in Naomi. She started walking towards me. She put her hand on my shoulder.

"MiMi, you have to learn to wake up. Big girls don't pee on themselves while they sleep. You are almost six years old now!" she said.

Just like I thought, no more tears, there were no more to cry. I waited, silently. She moved her hand, my shoulder warm from her touch. I knew this was it; she was going to hit me. I heard her pull the zipper down on the back of my dress. The air hit my naked back and made it sting. I felt her hands tugging the dress off my shoulders and down my waist, letting it fall to my ankles. We stood like that for a moment. I could feel her eyes piercing me.

"Take those wet panties off," Mama ordered as her footsteps made their way out of the room. I wasn't sure what was happening. *Was she going to whoop me naked?* I took my time removing my underwear. It hurt my stomach to bend down and I cringed as I pushed my panties down on top of the dress resting at my ankles. My panties were so big that I was able to step out of them along with the dress at the same time.

I heard bath water running in the next room. Mama came back in and started shuffling through the laundry hampers where we kept all of our clothes, both clean and dirty. She sniffed a pair of panties, and then pulled out one of her shirts. Finally she turned towards me.

She was acting very strangely. "MiMi, what are you just standing there for?" she asked with a puzzled look on her face. "Go get in the tub, baby."

I walked out of the room confused. Mama almost never ran my bath. Maybe she was going to whoop me in the tub. I caught a glimpse of myself in the bathroom mirror as I passed it. I wasn't surprised at what I saw, damage as usual. My legs didn't hurt that bad, so I lifted them easily over the side of the tub and sat in the really hot water without complaining. It was up to my waist. Mama came in and turned the water off. She sprinkled a white powder into the tub.

"This will make you feel better," she said softly. She sat on the toilet while she bathed me. I ignored the stinging sensation of my bruises as she washed me gently. She hummed the only Christian song I knew, "This Little Light of Mine."

"Lean back," she pushed me down in the water. It almost covered my entire head, but not quite. The warm soapy water stung as she poured it over my matted hair from a red 7'Eleven cup that she kept on the side of the tub. She never attempted to wash my face. She hummed softly the entire time.

"Are you hungry?" Mama asked as she dried me off and rubbed oil all over my body.

"Yes, Mommy," I felt so much love as she helped me into the clothes she put out for me. Her shirt was big enough to be a dress. It was hers and I was happy to wear it. I put the beating from that morning out of my head and fell into her arms as she hugged me and told me how much she loved me.

"What do you want to eat?"

"Umm, Umm. Cereal!" I exclaimed happily, "Captain Crunch Berries!"

Mama brushed my hair gently, "MiMi, you know cereal is for breakfast. Plus, you don't need all that sugar."

My heart sank with disappointment. Maybe I was asking for too much. "But, you can have it for dinner, just this one time." she said as she smiled at me, showing all of her teeth.

Everybody always said I had a pretty Mama and that I looked just like her, only darker. When she smiled, I thought she was pretty too. Mama showed all of her teeth when she smiled. I didn't. Her teeth were all even and much whiter than mine. Mama said when I grew up I would probably have her pretty teeth too, that pretty teeth ran in her daddy's family. She said that my chipped front tooth would fall out and come back in all pretty like hers one day. That's why we didn't get it fixed when she pushed me down the front porch steps and it broke.

Mama finished brushing my damp hair into a ponytail and I followed her into the kitchen. I sat on the empty milk crate next to the stove and chatted nonstop as she prepared my cereal. She placed the big, plastic, margarine bowl carefully on my lap and told me to be careful and not to drop it. I held onto the bowl tightly and enjoyed the grown up people cereal. This was exciting for me, to finally get some of Mama's special cereal.

I listened to Mama talk on the phone as I ate. She laughed and twisted her hair around her finger. I knew it was a man on the phone. Mama had mostly men friends. I had to call them all uncle so I wouldn't forget their names and get her in trouble.

"Yeah, I'll see you later tonight," I heard her say as she hung up the phone smiling her big smile again. I already knew what that meant. I was going to bed and Mama was having company.

Mama put me to bed early because I needed my rest. As though I didn't hear her making plans. She sprinkled the mattress with baby powder and laid a sheet over it from the hamper. She covered me with a thin holey blanket and gave me some medicine to help me sleep because I'd had a long day, she said. I heard a knock on the front door just as she was kissing me goodnight.

"Say your prayers. And don't forget to pray for Mama," she told me as she walked out the room, turning off the light and shutting the door behind her.

Mama was laughing and I could hear the two of them talking and tousling with each other, causing the raggedy sofa to creak. "Come on baby. You always teasing me," he said. Then I heard smacking, wet kissing sounds. A few minutes later, Mama opened the door to the room we shared and whispered out my name. I knew not to say anything because she thought I was already asleep. "Baby, get back in here," he barked at her sounding irritated, "Before I give both of y'all some."

"What you was about to say again?" she slammed the door closed and went back to confront him.

"Oh, pretty girl, I was just playing," he said laughing trying to lighten the tone of his voice.

I wondered what he had for me. What is *some* and why was Mama upset when he said he wanted to give me something too? She never got mad at any of the uncles. I fell asleep listening to him moan loudly, telling my Mama "That's it. Suck it real good, and daddy'll give you some of dis."

**Nakia R. Laushaul** was born in Los Angeles, California. She currently resides in Houston, Texas with her teenage son. In her spare time she enjoys reading, writing, and performing at local spoken word venues. She is currently working on her next project *Running from Solace*, a novel.

Rant it up with the author on her blog! Random Rants of Truth of a Social Butterfly: http://nakialaushaul.blogspot.com. Or visit her website www.nakiarlaushaul.com

Photo by: *Quyen Le*